MY FIRST GREEN COOK BOOK

DAVID ATHERTON

illustrated by ALICE BOWSHER

WALKER BOOKS

For my nieces and nephews, James, Louis, Mary-Joy, Charlotte. Joel and Benjamin.
Eat your greens! D.A.

For my Mum – thank you for always making a vegetarian option for me.
And for my Dad – thank you for trying my vegetarian cooking. A.B.

First published 2021 by Walker Books Ltd, 87 Vauxhall Walk, London SE11 5HJ

10 9 8 7 6 5 4 3 2 1

Text © 2021 Nomadbaker Ltd Illustrations © 2021 Alice Bowsher

"The Great British Bake Off" Baker logo™ is licensed by Love Productions Ltd

The right of David Atherton and Alice Bowsher to be identified as author and illustrator respectively of this work has been asserted by them in accordance with the Copyright, Designs and Patents Act 1988

This book has been typeset in Alice, Hunterswood, and Vibur Printed in China

British Library Cataloguing in Publication Data: a catalogue record for this book is available from the British Library

ISBN 978-1-5295-0060-8 www.walker.co.uk

All recipes are for informational and/or entertainment purposes only;
please check all ingredients carefully if you have any allergies, and if in doubt,

INTRODUCTION

My family is **vegetarian,** so I grew up eating food made with lots and lots of colourful vegetables. My mum – who's a fantastic cook – taught me that vegetarian food is easy to make and tastes delicious.

Thanks to my mum, I also learnt that adding vegetables, fruits and seeds to recipes can make them even more exciting. From cauliflower in your smoothie to pears in your muffins, or even chia seeds in your biscuits, this book is packed with recipes that have a tasty twist.

I've called this book a "green" cook book because "eating green" not only means eating things that are green in colour, but includes healthy vegetables, fruits and plants. AND we describe something as "green" if it is good for the planet too.

It's really important to learn about "eating green" and you can share the fun by doing the recipes with your friends and family. If you are already a star baker, or a fancy cook, you can also add your personal touches to the recipes and create your own flavour combinations.

So, tie on your apron, and let's get going on another food adventure!

David

CONTENTS

Yummy Meals

Savoury Snacks

Sweet Treats

Showstoppers

EATING GREEN

Home-grown food

Where does the food you eat come from? This is really important to think about when you're "eating green". If food travels a long way by plane or by lorry, it creates pollution, which is bad for our planet. Next time you buy fruits or vegetables, look where they've come from and ask whether you can buy locally produced alternatives. Or how about trying to grow your own?

Seasonal food

Another way to "eat green" is to eat fruits and vegetables that are in season. This means eating foods when they ripen naturally. For example, apples are ready to pick in the autumn and tomatoes are best in the summer. Food out of season has often travelled a long way; it might be full of pesticides or preservatives; and might have been stored for a long time. Choosing seasonal food when you can means that you're more likely to eat cleaner, healthier foods.

Top tip: *Did you know that lots of farms allow you to pick your own fruits and vegetables? See if you can find one close to you and pick your own food to eat!*

Healthy foods

We need to eat lots of different kinds of food to make sure we're as healthy as we can be. "Eating green" doesn't just mean 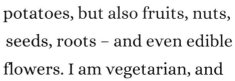 vegetables, like broccoli, carrots or potatoes, but also fruits, nuts, seeds, roots – and even edible flowers. I am vegetarian, and I still eat foods that come from animals such as eggs, milk or yogurt (I love yogurt). Some people are vegan, which means they don't eat any food that comes from an animal. Many of the recipes in this book are vegan and, for others, you can swap cow's milk for plant-based milk, butter for soy spread, cheese for vegan cheese and honey for agave, rice or date syrup.

Before you get going

- It takes time to learn how to be safe in the kitchen. All the recipes in this book will need adult supervision – work together and have fun!

- If you have food allergies, or are cooking for someone with food allergies, you need to check the ingredients list carefully.

- Finally, I am a nurse, so it is especially important for me to remind you to wash and dry your hands before cooking.

STORE CUPBOARD

A balanced diet includes carbohydrates, proteins, fats and fibre – as well as vitamins and minerals. I like to keep my store cupboard well-stocked with these ingredients to help me make nutritious and healthy recipes.

 Ground flaxseeds are shiny little seeds that are made into a powder. You can find them in your supermarket – sometimes called ground flaxseeds, ground linseeds or flax meal (but they are all the same thing).

Chia seeds are full of goodness, but they also go very sticky and soft when wet, which gives an important texture in baking.

 Nuts and seeds – take your pick! Sunflower seeds, flaked almonds and walnuts are all great for added protein, vitamins and fibre in your food.

 Flours come in many different varieties. In this book, you'll find plain, wholegrain, self-raising, buckwheat, strong white and brown bread flours. If you don't have room in your store cupboard, just stick to a good plain flour, a bread flour and a self-raising flour.

 Milk – the choice is yours. I usually use plant-based milks. The same goes for vegetable spreads or butters.

 Nut butters are full of good fats that we need in our diet. I love peanut butter, but there are lots of different nut butters such as cashew, almond or hazelnut.

 Tinned beans are a great source of vegetarian protein. They're full of fibre and B vitamins too.

 Grains like rice, wheat and oats contain carbohydrates that give you more energy. If you can, try whole grains like brown rice, which are more nutritious.

 Herbs and spices are a store cupboard must! Try different flavours and find your favourites. I love turmeric, paprika, oregano, cumin, cinnamon ... and more!

Weighing and measuring

- All recipes are measured in grams (g) and millilitres (ml)
- Tsp = teaspoon. Tbsp = tablespoon
- The oven temperatures are in degrees centigrade (°C). Increase the temperature by 20°C for a non fan-assisted oven.

A QUICK KIT LIST

It's a good idea to check you have all the equipment needed for a recipe before you start.
This is the equipment you will use in this book:

Baking paper   Baking tray   Beaker   Biscuit cutters   Blender

Cake tins   Child's safety knife   Chopping board   Cooling rack   Cupcake tray (12-hole)

Electric whisk   Food processor   Frying pan (non-stick)   Grater   Large mixing bowl

Measuring jug   Measuring spoons   Muffin tray (12-hole)   Oven gloves   Ovenproof dish

Peeler

Rolling pin   Saucepan   Sieve   Spatula

Spoon   Stick blender   Weighing scales   Whisk   Wok

YUMMY MEALS

MAGIC TOMATO SAUCE

This is my favourite sauce ever! It's so fresh and full of tasty vegetables. It can be used in all sorts of recipes – that's why it's magic! I make a fresh batch every week, then keep it in the fridge or freeze it. It's the perfect sauce for pasta, pizza and so many meals.

Ingredients

2 tins of chopped tomatoes (2 x 400g)

50ml water

1 onion

1 medium carrot

2 sticks of celery

½ a green pepper

5 cloves of garlic

1 tsp table salt

Makes 2 portions

Method

1 Tip both tins of tomatoes into a saucepan and add 50ml water. Bring to a simmer over a medium heat.

2 Peel the onion and carrot and roughly chop, along with the celery and pepper, then add to the saucepan.

3 Finely grate the garlic and add this to the saucepan with the salt.

4 Simmer for 30 minutes over a medium heat.

5 Pour into a blender and whizz until smooth. Leave to cool.

6 Divide into 2 portions and keep in the fridge for up to 3 days, or freeze.

SPAGHETTI "BOLOGNESE"

This dish gets its name from a beautiful city in Italy called Bologna. Everyone has their own special recipe – and this is mine. Spaghetti is fun to eat as it is long, slippery and slurpy, but there are lots of different pasta shapes and all of them go well with this delicious sauce.

Method

1 Add 1 portion of magic tomato sauce to a saucepan.

2 Add the lentils and oregano. Simmer over a low heat for 20 minutes, stirring frequently.

3 While your sauce is cooking, bring a large pan of water to the boil, add the spaghetti and simmer for 8–10 minutes. Then drain.

4 Serve the spaghetti with your "bolognese" sauce and grated cheese.

Ingredients

1 portion of magic
   tomato sauce (p. 12)
120g split red lentils
   (or cooked green lentils)
1 tsp dried oregano
200g spaghetti
40g Cheddar cheese, grated

Makes 4 servings

EYE LOVE "VEGGY" BREAD

Ingredients

375g strong white
    bread flour, plus
    extra for dusting
1 tsp fast-action yeast
1 tsp table salt
1 small carrot
240ml warm water
100g Cheddar cheese
4 medium eggs

Makes 4 servings

This recipe is from one of my favourite countries – Georgia. It is a bread called *khachapuri*, shaped like an eye with an egg in the middle. Have a look on the next page for some ideas to make your own version of this delicious "veggy" bread! Remember, dough needs a warm place and plenty of time to rise, so find a good book to read, and relax for a bit. This tasty bread is worth the wait and makes a perfect lunch or dinner.

Serving Suggestion

Serve your "veggy" bread with a delicious rainbow salad (p. 22) on the side.

Method

1 Put the flour, yeast and salt into a large mixing bowl.

2 Finely grate the carrot and add to the flour. Pour in the warm water.

3 Mix with a spatula until it forms a sticky dough.

4 Cover with a tea towel and leave for 5 minutes.

5 Knead for 5 minutes. It might be very sticky, but don't worry, (and don't add more flour).

6 Cover and leave in a warm place until it doubles in size (this may take more than an hour).

7 Preheat oven to 200°C (fan-assisted).

8 Split the dough into 4 pieces. On a lightly floured surface, roll each one out to make a rectangle about 25cm x 20cm in size.

9 Roll the longer edge over once on each side and press the ends together to make an eye shape.

10 Repeat with the other balls of dough, then transfer to a lined baking tray. Coarsely grate the cheese on top.

11 Cover and leave to rise for 20 minutes.

12 Bake for 8 minutes, then remove from the oven and crack an egg into each base.

13 Pop the bread back into the oven for 5 minutes until the egg is perfectly cooked.

Suggestions for fillings

Try adding your favourite veggies. Prepare your vegetables and oven-roast in a little oil for 20 minutes or until soft. Add to your bread base after step 11. You can try different fillings for each one – I like roasted peppers and mushrooms!

CHEESY NUTTY GNUDI

Gnudi (you don't pronounce the "g" like in the word "gnome") are Italian dumplings that taste like fluffy, cheesy clouds. I like to serve mine with my homemade, nutty heeeeey pesto! and a delicious green salad on the side.

Ingredients

2 medium eggs

160g ricotta cheese

60g vegetarian Parmesan (or pecorino), grated

60g plain flour, plus extra for dusting

½ a jar of heeeeey pesto! sauce (p. 34)

Makes 14 dumplings (2-4 servings)

Method

1 Whisk the eggs with a fork in a mixing bowl, then stir in the ricotta and Parmesan cheese.

2 Add the flour until just combined (do not over mix).

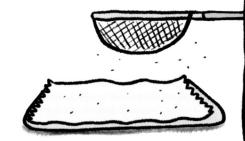

3 Line a baking tray with baking paper and dust with lots of flour using a sieve.

4 Place teaspoonfuls of the mixture (about the size of golf balls) on the baking tray.

5 Sprinkle more flour on top, then place in the fridge for 30 minutes.

6 Bring a large saucepan of water to the boil.

7 Gently drop each gnudi into the boiling water, cooking about six at a time. Once they float to the top, they are cooked. Use a slotted spoon to scoop each batch onto a plate. Repeat until all the gnudi are cooked, then return them to the pan, stir in the pesto and serve in bowls.

Serving suggestion

You can also serve the gnudi with magic tomato sauce (p. 12) and a sprinkle of cheese on top.

STIR-FRY NOODLES

I love stir-fry because it has oodles of soft noodles, crunchy vegetables and a tasty, sticky sauce. You can choose whatever vegetables you like, but ones with a good crunch work best. My favourite part of this recipe is shaking up the sauce and dancing around the kitchen! A perfect speedy-supper!

Ingredients

Sauce

1 clove of garlic, minced

20ml soy sauce

2 tbsp hoisin sauce

1 tbsp runny honey

1 tbsp nut butter

Stir-fry

1 red pepper

80g baby sweetcorn

2 tbsp vegetable oil,
   for frying

200g egg noodles

50g frozen peas

100g mangetout

1 small bunch of fresh
   coriander or basil

Makes 4 servings

Method

1 Put all of the sauce ingredients into a jar.

2 Screw on the lid and shake up and down until mixed!

3 Slice the red pepper into strips.

4 Slice the baby corn into quarters.

5 Add the oil to a wok (or frying pan) over a medium-high heat.

6 Add the pepper and baby sweetcorn to the wok and cook for 5 minutes, stirring every 30 seconds.

7 Cook the noodles according to the instructions on the packet, and add the peas to cook with them.

8 Add the mangetout to the wok and cook for another 2 minutes.

9 Drain the noodles and peas, then add to the wok and stir in. Add the sauce.

10 Pick the coriander or basil leaves and add. Keep stirring and fry for a final minute before serving.

Ingredients

100g spinach

350ml warm water

120g buckwheat flour

60g plain flour

1 tsp fast-action yeast

1 medium egg

10ml olive oil,
   for frying

Makes 8 pancakes

Suggestions for fillings

Try spreading some heeeeey pesto (p. 34), creamy beany dip (p. 38) or pea-camole (p. 39) onto the pancakes, then add grated cheese and chopped tomatoes or steamed broccoli.

GREEN SPINACH PANCAKES

When you mix all of these ingredients together, you'll get a bowl of bubbling green batter, just like a witch's cauldron. This isn't a deadly potion though – it's a fantastic pancake mixture! My favourite way to eat these is with hummus and grated carrot, rolled up into a sausage, but you can try any filling you like.

Method

1 Put the spinach and water in a jug and whizz with a stick blender until it looks like green water.

2 In a mixing bowl, add the flours, yeast, egg and the green water. Whisk until you have a smooth batter.

3 Cover and leave for 1 hour, until the batter looks bubbly.

4 Brush a frying pan with a little oil. Heat over a medium-high heat and pour in a ladle of batter.

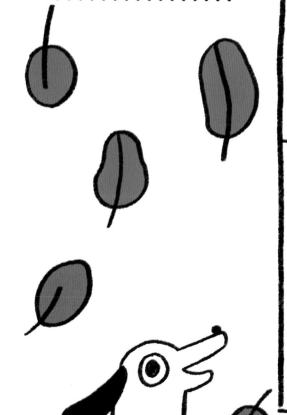

5 Allow to cook for 2 minutes, then, using a spatula, flip the pancake and cook for 2 minutes on the other side.

6 Transfer to a plate, fry the next pancake and keep stacking.

7 Serve your pancakes with different savoury fillings!

RAINBOW SALAD

This crunchy salad is packed with colourful and tasty ingredients, and it's delicious tossed in a mango dressing. If you have any dressing left over, pour it into a jar and pop it in the fridge (it lasts for up to a week). I also like to dunk carrot and pepper slices into the dressing as a healthy go-to snack.

Ingredients

Rainbow salad

½ a romaine lettuce

½ a red pepper

1 small carrot

40g Red Leicester cheese

100g tinned kidney beans

50g tinned sweetcorn

Mango dressing

100g mango, peeled and diced

10ml white wine vinegar

1 tsp table salt

1 tbsp runny honey

½ a clove of garlic, minced

Makes 4 servings

Method

1 Wash the lettuce, pepper and carrot in a colander.

2 Shake the lettuce dry, finely chop and transfer to a bowl.

3 Dice the cheese and the red pepper into little cubes and add to the bowl.

4 Peel and grate the carrot and add to the salad.

5 Drain the beans and sweetcorn and tip into the bowl.

6 To make the dressing, put all the ingredients in a beaker and blitz with a stick blender until smooth.

7 Toss the salad together with the dressing and serve.

SWEETCORN POTATO CAKES

My mum made these potato cakes when I was little and I loved
eating them with almost ALL of my meals. What will you eat them with?
Poached egg, mango chutney and steamed broccoli? Veggie sausages and beans?
Make the cakes into any shape you like. I do heart shapes because
I ♥ them and I think you will too!

Ingredients

1 medium carrot
   (about 100g)
450g King Edward
   potatoes
60g couscous
70ml water (boiling)
325g tinned sweetcorn
   (drained)
1 tsp table salt
1 tsp smoked paprika
1 medium egg
100g vegetarian
   Parmesan (or pecorino)
A little flour, for dusting

Makes 12 cakes

Method

1 Peel and dice the carrot and potatoes, then boil in a saucepan for 10–15 minutes.

2 Put the couscous into a bowl and pour over 70ml of boiling water. Leave for 5 minutes.

3 Put half the sweetcorn into a food processor and blitz until roughly chopped up.

4 Drain the carrot and potatoes and roughly mash.

5 In a mixing bowl, add the blended sweetcorn, mashed carrots and potatoes, couscous, salt, smoked paprika, whole sweetcorn and egg. Stir until combined.

6 Grate the cheese and add to the mixture.

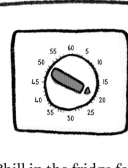

7 Chill in the fridge for 20 minutes.

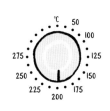

8 Preheat oven to 200°C (fan-assisted).

9 Press out the potato mix on a lightly floured surface to 2cm thick.

10 Create shapes with your hands or a biscuit cutter, and place the cakes on a lightly floured baking tray.

11 Bake for 15–20 minutes, then leave to cool for 5 minutes before serving with your favourite meal.

VEGGIE BURGERS

Ingredients

100g tinned black
    beans (drained)

110g sweet potato
    (uncooked)

100g firm tofu

50g Cheddar cheese

2 tbsp strong white
    bread flour, plus
    extra for dusting

½ tsp table salt

1 tsp ground cumin

½ tsp garam masala

1 medium egg

10ml olive oil, for frying

Makes 10 burgers

These scrummy burgers are packed with protein and taste AMAZING with a slice of melted cheese on top. Impress your friends at a BBQ and serve them in a burger bun with the "best" sweet potato fries (p. 50) on the side. Or just eat them as a midweek treat – heaven on a plate!

Method

1 In a large mixing bowl, crush the black beans with your hands to break them up.

2 Peel and finely grate the uncooked sweet potato.

3 Mash the tofu with a fork.

4 Grate the Cheddar cheese.

5 Add the cheese, tofu and sweet potato to the beans, then add the flour, salt, cumin, garam masala and egg.

6 Mix until well combined and then chill in the fridge for 30 minutes.

7 Divide the mixture into 40g portions. Roll each portion into a ball and press flat into a burger shape.

8 Put the burgers on an baking tray lined with baking paper and dust with flour. Then chill in the fridge for 1 hour.

9 Add the olive oil to a frying pan over a medium heat and gently fry the burgers on each side for 10 minutes.

10 Serve with your favourite sauce inside a burger bun and the "best" sweet potato fries on the side.

Ingredients

1 medium sweet potato

2 peppers (you choose
the colour)

1 small courgette

1 portion of magic tomato
sauce (p. 12)

1 can of coconut milk

1 tsp turmeric

1 tsp table salt

200g basmati rice

2 tsp garam masala

1 small bunch of fresh
coriander

Mango chutney, to serve

Makes 4 servings

CURRY KORMA BOWL

Some people like their curry hot and some people like
it mild. This is traditionally a mild, creamy curry (just
how I like it) but if you prefer it spicy, throw in some
chilli or add hot sauce at the end. Either way, it will
taste simply delicious!

Method

1 Peel the sweet potato, then chop the peppers, courgette and sweet potato into 1cm chunks.

2 Place the tomato sauce, coconut milk, turmeric and salt in a medium saucepan and bring to a simmer.

3 Add the sweet potato, peppers and courgette to the curry sauce and gently simmer for 30 minutes until the vegetables are cooked through.

4 Meanwhile, place the rice into a small saucepan over a medium heat and cover with boiling water, so it's 1cm above the rice level.

5 As soon as you see the first bubbles of a simmer, put on a tight-fitting lid and turn down the heat to the lowest setting. Leave the rice to cook for 12 minutes (do not remove the lid).

6 Take the curry off the heat and stir through the garam masala.

7 Cut the coriander with scissors (including the stalks).

8 Serve the rice in bowls, topped with the curry, and sprinkled with coriander. I like to serve mine with a big dollop of mango chutney too!

SPOOKY CARROT SOUP

This soup is the perfect treat for a chilly autumn day. It is sweet and smooth, with a spooky spider-web topping. If you don't like spiders, the yogurt topping can look really pretty as a swirl. My speckled scones (p. 40) or bread crowns (p. 48) are perfect for dipping in the soup too!

Ingredients

400g carrots

2 tsp olive oil

½ tsp table salt

1 portion of magic
   tomato sauce (p. 12)

1 litre of water

80g plain live yogurt

A squeeze of lemon
   (to taste)

A small packet of
   pumpkin seeds

Makes 4 servings

Method

1 Preheat oven to 200°C (fan-assisted).

2 Peel the carrots and cut into 1cm rounds.

3 Add the carrots to a baking tray with the oil and salt, and toss until coated.

4 Roast the carrots for 30 minutes until soft.

Pour the tomato sauce

6 Put the roasted carrots and hot tomato sauce into a blender and

7 Spoon the yogurt into a piping or sandwich bag, add a squeeze of lemon and mix it in.

8 Pour the soup into bowls then snip off a corner of the piping or sandwich bag and create a swirl on top of the soup.

9 Take a cocktail stick and drag lines from the centre of the swirl out to the edges to create the web.

10 Add pumpkin seed "flies" to your web. Serve with a witch's cackle and a speckled scone or bread crown.

Ingredients

1 large sweet potato
(about 250g)

200g cauliflower

200g broccoli

250g pasta
(macaroni or small shells)

20g butter

30g plain flour

450ml milk

100g Cheddar cheese, grated

½ tsp table salt

½ tsp garam masala

½ tsp smoked paprika
(optional)

Makes 6 servings

CHEESY VEGGIE BAKE

This creamy, cheesy and veggie-packed bake is the perfect comfort food. It makes you happy and warm when you eat it. I like to use broccoli, cauliflower and sweet potato in this dish, but you can choose your favourite vegetables. If you don't use all the cauliflower, why not try my cauli hot wings recipe on page 44?

Method

1 Peel and chop the sweet potato into 2cm chunks and cut the cauliflower and broccoli into small florets.

2 Add the vegetables to a large saucepan along with the pasta. Cover with plenty of boiling water and simmer for 10 minutes.

3 Drain everything and place the veggies and pasta in an ovenproof dish.

4 Preheat oven to 200°C (fan-assisted).

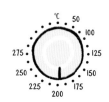

5 Melt the butter in a saucepan over a low heat. Add the flour, stirring with a whisk for 1 minute until combined.

6 Add 100ml of the milk and whisk to bring the mixture together (don't worry if it goes lumpy).

7 Turn up to a medium heat. As the sauce thickens, add more milk and keep whisking until you have used all the milk and the lumps are gone.

8 Add 70g of the grated cheese to the sauce along with the salt and garam masala. Combine together with the whisk.

9 Pour the sauce over the pasta and vegetables, sprinkle the rest of the cheese (and smoked paprika, if you are using) on top.

10 Bake for 15–20 minutes until it is golden and bubbling on top.

11 Once out of the oven, allow to cool for 5 minutes before serving.

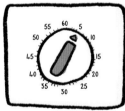

HEEEEEY PESTO!

Pesto is a brilliant way of adding flavour to almost any meal or snack. I like spreading it on sandwiches, tossing it through pasta, dolloping it on cheese scones or splattering it over pancakes – and more! Try different nuts and herbs to find your favourite pesto mix.

Ingredients

1 clove of garlic, minced

30g nuts (your choice, but I love walnuts, pistachios or cashews)

30g vegetarian Parmesan (or pecorino)

50ml olive oil

40g bunch of fresh basil

20g spinach

Makes 1 small jar

Method

1 Put the garlic, nuts and cheese into a food processor and whizz until the nuts are really broken up.

2 Add the olive oil and whizz again until it forms a paste.

3 Add the basil (stalks as well) and the spinach, then pulse until smooth (but so that you can still see bits of leaves). Pour into a jar and keep in the fridge for up to 3 days.

Serving suggestions

Serve with gnudi (p. 16), in your pancakes (p. 20), in your birds' nests (p. 45) or even as a sandwich spread (p. 48).

gnudi

pancakes

birds' nests

sandwich spread

SAVOURY SNACKS

CHEESY RABBIT BISCUITS

Ingredients

60g butter

120g plain flour,
   plus extra for dusting

20g wholemeal flour

80g Cheddar cheese

20g chia seeds

20 currants, for decoration

Makes 20 biscuits

These biscuits are deliciously cheesy with a golden crunch. A perfect snack for afternoon munching! I love making these rabbit shapes with big ears to scoop up my two favourite dips (pp. 38–39). You can try lots of different shapes too – what will you make?

Method

1 Cut the butter into cubes then rub into the flours until it resembles breadcrumbs.

2 Grate in the cheese.

3 Add the chia seeds.

4 Mix everything together until it forms a dough. You might need to sprinkle in a little water if the mixture is very dry, but be careful not to add too much.

5 Wrap and chill in the fridge for 30 minutes.

6 Preheat oven to 180°C (fan-assisted).

7 On a lightly floured surface, roll out the dough to at least 0.5cm thick (or thicker, if you prefer).

8 Cut out the biscuits with a small person biscuit cutter (10cm). Fold in the arms and transfer to a lined baking tray. The legs are now your bunny ears!

9 Cut the currants in half and put 2 halves in each biscuit for the eyes, just below the ears.

10 Bake for 12–15 minutes, then allow to cool. Serve with some yummy dips!

CREAMY BEANY DIP

This dip can be made with lots of different beans. Have fun and experiment! Kidney beans will give you a pink dip, and black beans will make it black. The important thing to remember is to whizz, whizz, whizz until the dip is smooth and creamy. Serve with carrot sticks, cheesy rabbit biscuits (p. 36), or bread crowns (p. 48)!

Ingredients

½ a clove of garlic

400g tin of cannellini
    beans (drained)

100g cottage cheese

½ tsp smoked paprika

30g light tahini
    (or olive oil)

1 tsp table salt

Makes 1 big bowl

Method

1 Crush the garlic and transfer to a food processor.

2 Add the rest of the ingredients to the food processor and whizz until smooth.

3 Serve with your choice of crunchy vegetables or biscuits and enjoy!

PEA-CAMOLE

Guacamole is a Mexican dish and is known for its very strong flavours. This version includes petits pois, small, sweet peas; which makes it smooth and sweet. It's perfect for dipping with cheesy biscuits and it makes a great sandwich spread too!

Ingredients

100g frozen petits pois

1 large avocado

½ tsp table salt

20ml olive oil

½ lime, juiced

A small bunch of
   fresh coriander

Makes 1 big bowl

Method

1 Put the frozen petits pois into a bowl and cover with boiling water. Leave for 3 minutes.

2 Drain the peas and tip into a blender.

3 Carefully cut the avocado in half, peel and remove the stone.

4 Add half the avocado to the blender, along with the salt, oil and lime juice. Whizz until smooth.

5 Mash the other avocado half on a plate with a fork.

6 Mix it all together in a bowl. Chop the coriander leaves and sprinkle on top.

Ingredients

400g self-raising flour,
   plus extra for dusting

1 tsp baking powder

½ tsp table salt

20g poppy seeds

85g unsalted butter

1 ripe plantain

70g Cheddar cheese

170ml milk (plus a little
   extra to brush the scones)

Makes 25 scones

SPECKLED SCONES

These cheesy scones are beautifully soft and speckled with poppy seeds. I make mine with plantain, a special type of banana popular in Africa and the Caribbean. Once the scones have cooled, split them in half and spread a little butter on them, or dunk them into some spooky carrot soup (p. 30).

Method

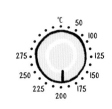

1 Preheat oven to 200°C (fan-assisted).

2 Put the flour, baking powder, salt and poppy seeds into a bowl.

3 Cut the butter into cubes then rub into the flour mix until it resembles breadcrumbs.

 **4** Coarsely grate the plantain and cheese, then stir into the flour mixture.

 **5** Stir in the milk and bring it together to form a ball of dough (don't worry if it is a little sticky).

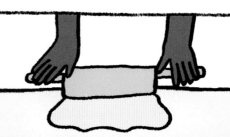 **6** On a lightly floured surface, roll out the dough until it is 1.5cm thick.

 **7** Cut out the scones with a 5cm biscuit cutter and place on a lined baking tray.

 **8** Continue until you've used up all the dough (about 25 scones).

10 Bake for 8–10 minutes, then leave to cool before eating.

 **9** Brush the tops of the scones with the extra milk.

CRESCENT MOON PIES

These yummy pies are made with sweet potato, but you can try lots of different fillings. What about roasted peppers and chickpeas? Or carrots and potatoes? You can experiment with more or less garam masala and try other spices like curry powder for something a little hotter.

Ingredients

50g unsalted butter

120g plain flour,
   plus extra for dusting

30g wholemeal plain flour

1 medium sweet potato

1 medium egg

200g tinned sweetcorn
   (drained)

1 tsp garam masala

½ tsp table salt

10ml olive oil, for frying

20g poppy seeds

Makes 14 pies

Method

1 Cut the butter into cubes and then, with your fingers, rub into the two flours until it resembles breadcrumbs.

2 Peel and finely grate the sweet potato and add 50g to the flour mix.

3 Crack the egg over a clean bowl and tip the yolk from shell to shell, letting the egg white run into the bowl (save this for later). Add the yolk to the flour mixture.

4 Bring the flour mixture into a dough (add a little water if necessary, but not too much).

5 Wrap and chill in the fridge for 30 minutes.

6 Add the rest of the sweet potato, sweetcorn, garam masala and salt to a frying pan with a little oil over a low heat. Cook for 10 minutes, stirring every minute.

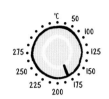

7 Preheat oven to 180°C (fan-assisted).

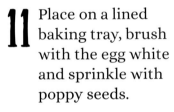

8 Roll out the dough to at least 0.5cm thick (a bit thinner if you can), then cut out circles with a 10cm biscuit cutter.

9 Put a teaspoon of sweet potato mix from the frying pan in the middle of each circle.

10 Fold each circle over and press gently to seal. Crimp the edges with a fork.

11 Place on a lined baking tray, brush with the egg white and sprinkle with poppy seeds.

12 Bake for 15 minutes, leave to cool then serve!

Ingredients

250g cauliflower

30g plain flour

2 tbsp milk

2 tbsp water

½ tsp smoked paprika

¼ tsp table salt

50g breadcrumbs

Makes 4 servings

CAULI HOT WINGS

These cauliflower bites have the perfect crunch and are just as delicious as chicken hot wings. Add them as a tasty side dish to a meal, or munch them as a snack with some pea-camole (p. 39).

Method

1 Preheat oven to 180°C (fan-assisted).

2 Cut the cauliflower into little florets.

3 To make the batter, put the flour, milk, water, smoked paprika and salt into a bowl and mix until smooth.

4 Tip the breadcrumbs onto a plate.

5 Dip the florets into the batter, then roll in the breadcrumbs.

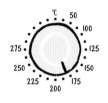

6 Place the florets on a lined baking tray (make sure they're not touching) and bake for 20 minutes.

7 Give your florets a little shake and turn them over with tongs.

8 Bake again for 15 minutes.

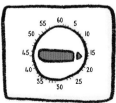

9 Serve your cauli hot wings with your favourite dip!

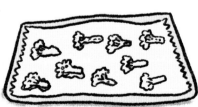

BIRDS' NESTS

Tweet, tweet! You'll have loads of fun making these super-easy birds' nests. The filo pastry makes the base really crispy and crunchy, and the mini mozzarella balls look like tiny eggs, just like in a real nest.

Ingredients

5ml vegetable oil,
   for greasing

4 sheets of filo pastry

8 tbsp of heeeeey
   pesto! (p. 34)

8 cherry tomatoes

16 mini mozzarella balls

Makes 8 nests

Method

1 Preheat oven to 150°C (fan-assisted).

2 Brush 8 holes of a 12-hole muffin tin with vegetable oil.

3 Roll the 4 filo pastry sheets into a sausage shape.

4 Carefully, with a sharp knife, cut slices that are 0.5cm thick.

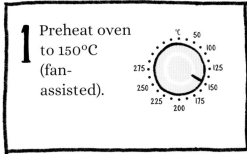

5 Tease out the filo strands so they look like spaghetti. Divide into 8 portions.

6 Tangle the filo strands together to make 8 nests. Make a big hollow in the middle of the nests and put in the muffin tin.

7 Bake for 8 minutes.

8 Dribble the inside of each nest with a tablespoon of pesto, add a tomato and 2 mini mozzarella balls. You're ready to serve your nests!

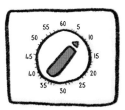

MINI PIZZA SWIRLS

Ingredients

300g strong white bread flour,
  plus extra for dusting

50g strong brown bread flour

1 tsp instant yeast

1 tsp table salt

200ml warm water

10ml olive oil, for greasing

40g tomato puree

30ml water

1 tsp dried oregano

80g Cheddar cheese

Makes 10–12 pizzas

These mini pizza swirls are much easier to carry around than a big flat, floppy pizza, so they're perfect for a lunch box, or a snack to take on the go. Have a look on the next page for suggestions for extra fillings. YUM!

Method

1 In a mixing bowl, combine the flours, yeast, salt and water until it forms a dough. Cover and allow to sit for 10 minutes.

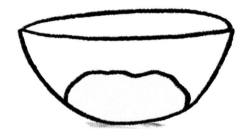

2 Knead the dough on a lightly floured surface for 5 minutes (do not add lots of flour, it doesn't matter if it starts off sticky).

3 Place the dough in a clean bowl and cover with a tea towel. Leave in a warm place until it doubles in size (about 25 minutes).

4 Lightly grease a 12-hole muffin tin.

5 Press the air out of the dough. Roll it out to make a rectangle about 30cm x 20cm in size.

6 Mix the tomato puree, 30ml of water and oregano until combined, then spread onto the dough.

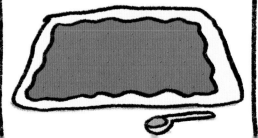

Suggestions for fillings

Once you get to step 7, sprinkle on your favourite veggies. Why not try thin slices of mushrooms or even grated carrot?

7 Grate the cheese and sprinkle on top. You can add any extra veggies now!

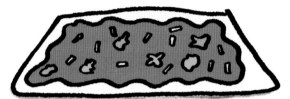

8 Roll the dough up into a long sausage and then cut into 10 pieces.

9 Arrange each piece in one of the holes of the muffin tin, cover and leave in a warm place until it doubles in size (about 25 minutes).

10 Preheat oven to 200°C (fan-assisted)

11 Sprinkle with a little extra cheese and bake for 12 minutes. Allow to cool a little before serving.

BREAD CROWNS

Ingredients

300g strong white
   bread flour, plus
   extra for dusting

50g strong brown
   bread flour

1 tsp fast-action yeast

½ tsp ground turmeric

1 tsp table salt

200ml warm water

Makes 8 crowns

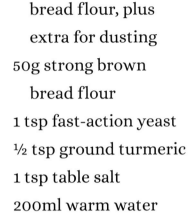

If I was going to crown the queen of all food, it would be bread – I eat bread every day (usually with peanut butter) – so I wanted to make bread fitting for royalty. Turmeric is a spice that is good for you, and when added to bread dough it turns really yellow, which is perfect for a crown.

Method

1 Mix the flours, yeast, turmeric, salt and water together until it forms a dough.

2 Cover with a tea towel and allow to sit for 10 minutes.

3 Knead the dough on a lightly floured surface for 5 minutes (it doesn't matter if it starts off sticky – don't add too much flour).

4 Cover with a tea towel and leave in a warm place until it doubles in size (about 1 hour).

5 Divide the dough into 8 pieces and roll into balls.

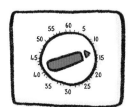

6 Stick 2 fingers through the middle of each ball, then stretch your fingers apart to open up the hole.

7 Spin the circle of dough on your fingers to open up the hole to about 4cm wide.

8 Put on a lined baking tray, cover and leave to rise until it doubles in size (about 30 minutes).

9 Preheat oven to 200°C (fan-assisted).

10 Use scissors to snip all around the ring.

11 Bake for 12 minutes and leave to cool.

12 Serve with spooky carrot soup (p. 30), or heeeeey pesto (p. 34) and cheese, or your yummy dips (pp. 38–39).

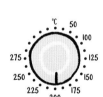

THE "BEST" SWEET POTATO FRIES

Ingredients

2 medium sweet potatoes

1 tbsp cornflour

½ tsp table salt

2 tbsp vegetable oil

½ tsp smoked paprika
  (optional)

Makes 4 servings

Who wants normal fries when you can have the "best" sweet potato fries?! These are perfect as a snack or as part of a main meal. Be careful: if you cook these too close together, they go soft, and we want them crispy!

Method

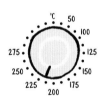

1 Preheat oven to 220°C (fan-assisted).

2 Peel the sweet potatoes and cut into 5cm strips.

3 Toss in a large mixing bowl with the cornflour, salt and oil.

4 Spread the fries onto a lined baking tray and make sure they don't touch each other. Use two trays if necessary.

5 Cook for 20 minutes and then check the fries.

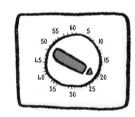

6 Shake the fries. If any are brown at the edges, move them to the middle of the tray.

7 Bake for another 10 minutes.

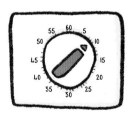

8 Once out of the oven, sprinkle with the smoked paprika. Perfect on their own, with dips (pp. 38–39) or a side to veggie burgers (p. 26).

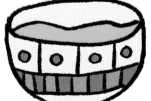

SWEET TREATS

SUPER STRAWBERRY JAM

My super strawberry jam is used in so many recipes in this book: in my jam tarts (p. 53), on top of rice pudding (p. 62), on my pink scones (p. 66) and spring butterfly cupcakes (p. 70) – but my favourite is spreading it on toast! This jam uses the magic of chia seeds, which go soft and sticky when wet.

Ingredients

400g strawberries
(or frozen fruit)

4 tsp caster sugar
(optional)

20g chia seeds

1 tsp lemon juice

Makes 1 jar

Method

1 Roughly chop the strawberries and put in a saucepan. Taste a little bit of strawberry to see how sweet it is.

2 Gently stir the strawberries over a low heat for 5 minutes. Take off the heat and crush with a potato masher.

3 Simmer for another 5 minutes. (If the strawberry didn't taste very sweet in step 1, add the sugar now).

4 Take off the heat. Stir in the chia seeds and lemon juice.

5 Allow to cool, then transfer to a jar with a lid.

6 Keep in the fridge and use within a week.

JAM TARTS

Ingredients

50g icing sugar

100g plain flour, plus extra
for dusting

60g plain wholemeal flour

80g unsalted butter

1 medium egg

Super strawberry jam

Makes 12 tarts

Here's a recipe for jam tarts, using – you guessed it – my super strawberry jam! Or you can try adding yogurt and fruit, chocolate spread and even peanut butter for the filling.

Method

1 Sift the icing sugar into a mixing bowl and add the flours. Cut the butter into cubes and then, with your fingers, rub into the flour mixture until it resembles breadcrumbs.

2 Crack the egg over a clean bowl and tip the yolk from shell to shell, letting the egg white run into the bowl. Add the yolk to the flour mix and combine until it forms a ball of dough.

3 Wrap and leave in the fridge for 30 minutes.

4 Preheat oven to 200°C (fan-assisted).

5 On a lightly floured surface, roll out the dough to 0.5cm thick. Cut out 12 discs with a 10cm biscuit cutter.

6 Place each disc in a hole in a 12-hole cupcake tray, then prick the base with a fork a few times.

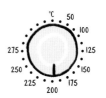

7 Chill in the fridge for 15 minutes.

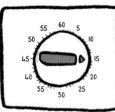

8 Bake for 15–20 minutes (until golden) then allow to cool before removing from the tin.

9 Spoon a teaspoonful of super strawberry jam into each pastry case.

APPLE ROCK CAKES

I used to love collecting apples when I was little, and these rock cakes were one of my favourite treats to bake. They stay fresh for a couple of days – in an airtight tub – and are easy to take on an apple-picking picnic adventure!

Ingredients

2 medium Bramley
    apples (150–200g)
180g self-raising flour
40g plain wholemeal flour
1 tsp baking powder
1 tsp ground cinnamon
50g caster sugar, plus extra
    for sprinkling
120g unsalted butter
20g raisins
1 medium egg
20ml milk
1 tsp vanilla extract

Makes 12 cakes

Method

1 Peel the apples, chop into 1cm pieces and put in a bowl of cold water.

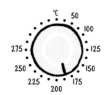

2 Preheat oven to 180°C (fan-assisted).

3 Put the flours, baking powder, cinnamon and sugar into a mixing bowl. Cut the butter into cubes and rub into the mixture until it resembles breadcrumbs.

4 Drain the apples and toss through the mixture with the raisins.

5 In a separate small bowl, mix the egg, milk and vanilla extract together with a fork.

6 Add the egg mixture to the dry mixture and bring together to form a dough.

7 Take big dessertspoonfuls of the mixture, then place on a lined baking tray and sprinkle with sugar.

8 Bake for 12–15 minutes, then allow to cool on a cooling rack.

CHOCOLATE COOKIES

Some cookies are crunchy, some are chewy and some melt in your mouth – just like these. Decorate them with chocolate chips and chewy raisins to make a treat full of avo-choco-goodness.

Ingredients

1 ripe avocado
   (about 100g)
100g soft brown sugar
15g ground flax meal
1 tsp vanilla extract
20g cocoa powder
50g plain flour
½ tsp bicarbonate
   of soda
30g raisins
40g milk chocolate chips

Makes 10 cookies

Method

1 Preheat oven to 180°C (fan-assisted).

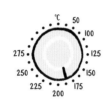

2 Carefully cut the avocado in half, peel and take out the stone. Add to a mixing bowl and whizz with a stick blender. Add the sugar, flax meal and vanilla extract and whizz again.

3 Add the cocoa powder, flour and bicarbonate of soda, and whizz until smooth.

4 Using a dessertspoon, place dollops of the mixture onto a lined baking tray. Press the back of the spoon on top of each dollop to make a circle.

5 Decorate with the raisins and chocolate chips.

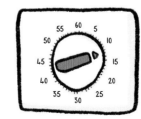

6 Bake for 12–15 minutes.

7 Cool on a cooling rack before eating – yum!

FREEZY GRAPES

These freezy treats taste just like sorbet. When you cover the grapes in yogurt and crunchy sprinkles, you get sour, sweet and juicy all in one bite! They're a refreshing summer snack, but I like to eat them all year round.

Method

1 Line a tray with baking paper.

2 Put a grape onto a cocktail stick and dip into the yogurt.

3 Sprinkle your freeze-dried strawberries (or edible decorations) over the yogurt-covered grape, rotating the cocktail stick as you go.

4 Gently place the grape on the tray and release it with another cocktail stick. Repeat with all the grapes.

5 Freeze overnight, then transfer to a freezer bag. Keep in the freezer and eat as an icy treat!

Ingredients

40 red grapes

115g pot of live strawberry yogurt

Freeze-dried strawberry pieces (or other edible sprinkles)

Makes 40 freezy grapes

LEMON & PEAR MUFFINS

These fruity, zesty muffins are so soft and fluffy, it's hard to eat only one at a time! I make mine with pears and lemon, but you could try swapping the lemon for a lime.

Ingredients

1 lemon

410g tin of pear halves in juice
   (225g of actual pears)

25g porridge oats

75g caster sugar

25g runny honey

40ml light olive oil

2 medium eggs

200g plain flour

50g plain wholemeal flour

2 tsp baking powder

10g poppy seeds

Extra caster or demerara
   sugar for sprinkling on top

Makes 12 muffins

Method

1 Zest the lemon and set the zest aside.

2 Juice the lemon into a small bowl. Add the juice from the tin of pears until you have 100g.

3 Add the lemon and pear juice to a small saucepan, along with the oats, and simmer gently for 3 minutes on the lowest heat until the oats are soft.

4 Preheat oven to 200°C (fan-assisted).

5 Put the oat mixture into a food processor with the pear halves, sugar, honey and oil, and blend until smooth.

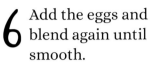

6 Add the eggs and blend again until smooth.

7 In a mixing bowl, combine the flours, baking powder, poppy seeds and lemon zest.

8 Pour the blended pear mixture into the flour mixture and stir until combined.

9 Prepare a 12-hole muffin tin with paper cases. Spoon the mixture into the paper cases until they're three-quarters full, then sprinkle with the extra sugar.

10 Bake for 5 minutes at 200ºC, then, after 5 minutes, drop the temperature to 180ºC and bake for a further 15 minutes. Leave to cool on a cooling rack, then serve.

STICKY FLAPJACK

Ingredients

100g butter

80g golden syrup

130g dates

50g dried apricots,
   chopped

50g raisins

50g flaked almonds

20g sunflower seeds

150g porridge oats

20g wholemeal flour

Makes 16 flapjacks

Who is Jack, and why is she flappy? I have no idea why this treat is called flapjack, but it's one of my faves. This version is super-sticky and chewy — just how I like it. For a special breakfast, I crumble the flapjack into a bowl of plain yogurt with some chopped fruit. Delicious!

Method

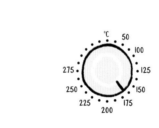

1 Preheat oven to 170°C (fan-assisted).

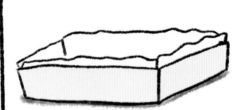

2 Line a 20cm square tin with baking paper.

3 Melt the butter and golden syrup in a small saucepan over a low heat.

4 Put the dates into a food processor, add the melted butter and syrup and blitz until smooth.

5 Add the apricots, raisins, almonds, sunflower seeds, oats and flour into a mixing bowl.

6 Pour in the sticky date mixture and stir with a spatula until everything is coated.

7 Tip into the tin and push down with a spatula until level.

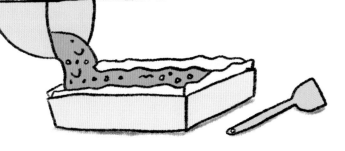

8 Bake for 25 minutes, until golden.

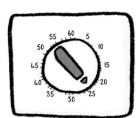

9 Allow to cool before removing from the tin and cutting into squares.

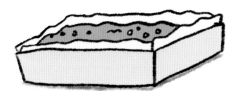

RICE PUDDING

I loved it when my grandma used to make me this delicious, comforting dish. She baked hers in the oven, but my version is stirred on the hob. Rice pudding is great just on its own, but I like to add honey and top it with a big dollop of my super strawberry jam (p. 52). Have a look on the next page for some ideas to tickle your taste buds.

Ingredients

80g pudding rice
   (or risotto rice)
600ml milk
100ml water
40g runny honey
Super strawberry jam,
   to serve

Makes 2 servings

Method

1 Add the rice, milk, water and honey to a medium saucepan and bring to a gentle simmer (small bubbles) while stirring.

2 Put a lid on the pan and simmer for 40 minutes, giving it a stir every 5 minutes. You might want to use a timer so you don't forget. Be careful it doesn't boil over!

3 If it gets too thick before 40 minutes is up, add some more milk. It should be gloopy, not solid.

4 Top with a big dollop of super strawberry jam and serve!

Try these tasty variations

Chocolatey rice pudding

Add 2 tsp cocoa powder and 1 tsp vanilla extract to the saucepan before simmering. Once served, drop a few squares of chocolate on top and wait for them to melt.

Tropical rice pudding

Add 30g dried mango and 10g desiccated coconut to the saucepan before simmering, and top with a fresh mango, peeled and chopped into chunks.

Spicy rice pudding

Add 10g raisins and 1 tsp ground cinnamon to the saucepan before simmering. When served, grate an apple on top and sprinkle with some demerara sugar.

ICE-DREAM SMOOTHIE

I dream of ice cream! You will be amazed that this is made from whizzed-up cauliflower. It's so creamy and the mango makes it super-sweet. You can try swapping the mango for other fruits like banana or pineapple. Or, why not try flavouring it with a little cordial?

Ingredients

1 mango
  (about 200g)
4 cauliflower florets
  (about 120g)
4 tbsp plain live yogurt
2 tsp runny honey
Fresh fruit, to serve

Makes 4 servings

Method

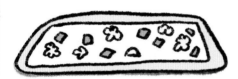

1 Peel the mango, then cut in half and remove the stone. Chop into 2cm chunks and place on a baking tray.

2 Add the cauliflower florets (don't use the stalky bits). Freeze for at least 3 hours (best frozen overnight).

3 Using a food processor, blend the frozen mango, cauliflower, yogurt and honey until smooth.

4 Transfer to bowls and top with fresh fruit. Yum!

POPPED CHOCS

Take some popcorn kernels (this is the name for a grain of corn), heat them in hot oil and – pipperty, popperty, pop – you have a pan full of soft, puffed popcorn. The only thing to make it more delicious is to cover it in chocolate, of course!

Ingredients

15ml vegetable oil

40g popcorn kernels

200g dark or plain chocolate

50g peanut butter

60g raisins (or other dried fruit)

30g unsalted peanuts

Makes 20 chocs

Method

1 Put the oil and 3 kernels in a saucepan over a medium heat. When they pop, put the rest of the kernels in and quickly put on a tight-fitting lid.

2 Wait until you can't hear any more popping then transfer to a mixing bowl.

3 Break up the chocolate and put into a heatproof bowl with the peanut butter.

4 Sit the bowl over a pan of barely simmering water and allow the chocolate to melt, stirring occasionally.

5 Pour the chocolate mixture onto the popcorn, and add the raisins and nuts. Give it a good stir.

6 Place dessertspoonfuls of the mixture onto a lined baking tray, then pop in the fridge to cool and set, before eating.

Ingredients

2 cooked beetroot
   (about 120g)

80ml milk

350g self-raising flour,
   plus extra for dusting

1 tsp baking powder

50g caster sugar

1 tsp vanilla extract

80g butter

To serve

Super strawberry jam

200g live Greek yogurt

200g strawberries

Icing sugar, to dust

Makes 12 scones

STRAWBERRY PINK SCONES

Everything looks better in pink! And these scones are no exception. They are perfect for an afternoon tea party and, served with your homemade super strawberry jam (p. 52), are sure to impress your friends!

Method

1 Finely grate the beetroot into a bowl and add the milk.

2 Add the flour, baking powder, sugar and vanilla extract to a large mixing bowl. Cut the butter into cubes and then, with your fingers, rub into the mix until it resembles breadcrumbs.

3 Pour in the milk and beetroot mixture.

4 Mix until it forms a dough and let it sit for 10 minutes.

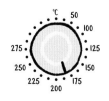

5 Preheat oven to 180°C (fan-assisted).

6 On a floured surface, roll out the dough until it is 2cm thick.

7 Cut out the scones using a large biscuit cutter.

8 Transfer to a lined baking tray and bake for 12–15 minutes.

9 Leave to cool on a cooling rack.

10 Slice the scones in half, spread with jam and put a dollop of yogurt in the middle.

11 Cut the strawberries into quarters and decorate each scone with three pieces.

12 Dust with the icing sugar to finish.

Ingredients

60g white chocolate

150g dried apricots

40g walnuts

30g desiccated coconut,
   plus extra for decoration

20g porridge oats

Makes 20 snowballs

NUTTY SNOWBALLS

These balls are small but give you a mighty burst of energy! If you're going to a dance class, cycling in the park or if you want to beat your friends in a snowball fight, then this is the snack for you!

Method

1 Break up the chocolate into a heatproof bowl and place over a pan of simmering water. Allow the chocolate to melt, stirring occasionally.

2 Blitz the apricots, walnuts and desiccated coconut in a food processor until it resembles breadcrumbs.

3 Add the melted white chocolate and blitz again until combined.

4 Transfer to a bowl and stir in the oats.

5 Take a teaspoon of the mixture and squeeze it together in your hands, then roll it into a ball.

6 Roll each ball in the extra desiccated coconut and place on a lined baking tray.

7 Once you've finished all the balls, chill in the fridge for 1 hour.

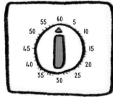

8 Once set, store your snowballs in a jar or tub and keep in the fridge to munch on as a snack!

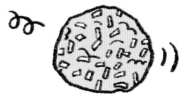

SHOWSTOPPERS

SPRING BUTTERFLY CUPCAKES

It takes a little bit of practice to make the wings on these pretty cupcakes look just like butterflies. I practised a lot and won 1st prize in a local baking competition when I was eight (which I'm still very proud of).

Ingredients

Cakes

170g frozen petits pois

100g unsalted butter (diced)

40g Greek yogurt

2 medium eggs

100g caster sugar

3 tsp vanilla extract

160g self-raising flour

1 tsp baking powder

Topping

130g unsalted butter
   (at room temperature)

1 tsp vanilla extract

250g icing sugar,
   plus extra for dusting

2 tbsp Greek yogurt

12 tsp super strawberry
   jam (p. 52)

Colourful edible sprinkles

Makes 12 cakes

Method

1 Simmer the frozen petits pois in boiling water for 5 minutes.

2 Drain the peas and leave them in a bowl of cold water for 5 minutes.

3 Preheat oven to 180°C (fan-assisted).

4 Prepare a a 12-hole cupcake tin with paper cases.

5 Drain the peas and whizz in a blender with the butter, yogurt, eggs, sugar and vanilla extract until smooth.

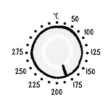

6 Sift the flour and baking powder into a bowl and add the mixture from the blender. Stir carefully until combined.

7 Divide the mixture between the paper cases (no more than two-thirds full).

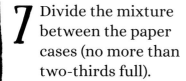

8 Bake for 15 minutes, then cool on a cooling rack.

9 For the icing, whisk the butter with the vanilla extract and icing sugar until smooth. Then mix in the Greek yogurt.

10 Once cool, cut out a circle from the top of each cake, leaving a small hole, and set aside.

11 Put a teaspoon of jam in each hole, followed by a generous dollop of the icing.

12 Cut the cake tops in half and stick them into the icing like butterfly wings. Dust with icing sugar and decorate with sprinkles.

SUMMER SANDCASTLE CAKE

Ingredients

Cake

200g caster sugar

200g soft brown sugar

300ml vegetable oil

6 medium eggs

320g peeled carrots
   (or parsnips)

340g plain flour

4 tsp baking powder

2 tsp cinnamon

Icing

100g unsalted butter
   (room temperature)

200g icing sugar

2 tsp vanilla extract

100g cream cheese
   (room temperature)

Toppings and decorations

100g digestive biscuits

About 12 toothpicks

100g marzipan

A small sheet of rice paper

Makes 14–16 servings

I grew up in a seaside town and loved going down to the beach to make sandcastles. The sand on this castle is made from whizzed up biscuits and inside is a delicious carrot cake.

Just like a sandcastle, you can choose to decorate as you like!

This is a BIG cake, so make sure you have a large mixing bowl.

Method

1 Preheat oven to 160°C (fan-assisted).

2 Grease and dust two 20cm round tins with a little flour. It helps to line the bottoms with baking paper too.

3 In a large mixing bowl, beat the sugars, oil and eggs until smooth.

4 Finely grate the carrots, add to the sugar mix and slowly fold in the flour, baking powder and cinnamon.

5 Divide the mixture between the two tins.

6 Bake both cakes for 40 minutes.

7 Turn the cakes out onto a cooling rack and leave to cool. Then put in the fridge for 20 minutes.

8 For the icing, cube the butter, add the icing sugar and beat together using an electric whisk.

9 When smooth, add the vanilla extract and half the cream cheese and mix until smooth. Then add the rest of the cream cheese and mix in.

10 Whizz the digestive biscuits in a food processor until the mixture looks like sand.

11 Neatly cut the edges off both cakes to make 2 squares (save the edges for your turrets).

12 Sandwich the cakes with about one-third of the icing. Spread another third of the icing all over the top and sides.

13 Sprinkle the digestive biscuits all over so it looks like a sandcastle.

14 Cut the leftover pieces of cake into turrets. Spread with the remaining icing, cover in biscuit "sand" and fix to your sandcastle using toothpicks.

15 Use marzipan to make shell decorations. Cut little triangles out of rice paper, moisten with some water and wrap them around the toothpicks to make flags.

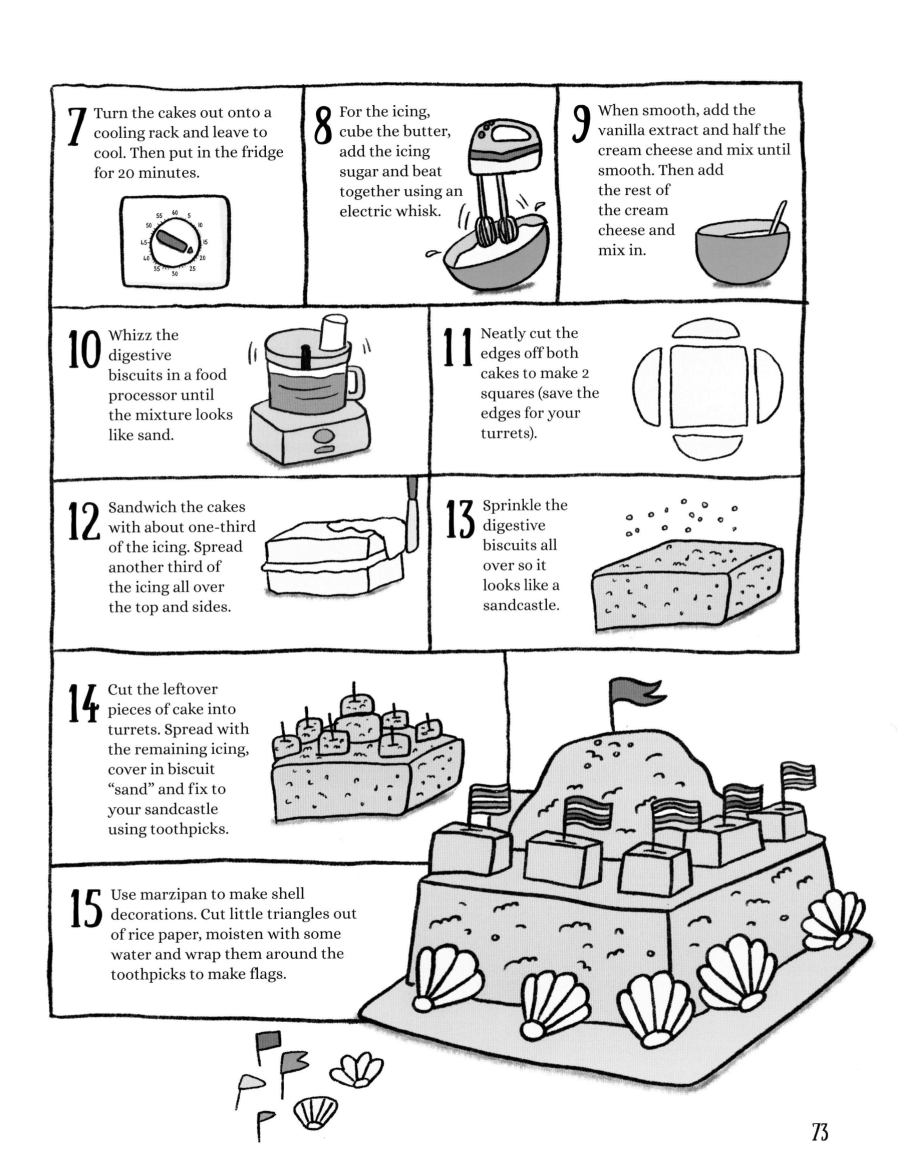

Ingredients

Cake

600g caster sugar

400g plain flour

40g cocoa powder

4 tsp baking powder

200ml milk

160ml vegetable oil

4 medium eggs

340ml water

2 tsp vanilla extract

1 tsp of peppermint extract

Middle Icing

1 large sweet potato
   (about 250g)

25g cocoa powder

1 tsp vanilla extract

80g icing sugar

Top Icing

150g caster sugar

60g cocoa powder

40g cornflour

180ml water

2 tsp vanilla extract

20g unsalted butter

Decorations

100g marzipan

6 raspberries

6 strawberries

Sprigs of fresh mint

Makes 14–16 servings

AUTUMN WOODLAND CAKE

I love going for walks in the forest and looking up at the trees. Now imagine if everything was made of chocolate?! This recipe gives you the basic forest floor, but you can make other edible plants, insects or leaves to create a woodland wonderland.

Method

1 Preheat oven to 160°C (fan-assisted).

2 Grease and dust two 20cm round tins with a little flour. It helps to line the bottoms with baking paper too.

3 In a large bowl, mix together the sugar, flour, cocoa powder and baking powder.

4 In a separate bowl, beat together the milk, oil, eggs, water, vanilla and peppermint extracts.

5 Pour the milk mix into the flour mix and beat until smooth.

6 Divide the mixture between the two tins and bake for 20–25 minutes (until a skewer comes out clean).

7 Allow the cakes to cool, then chill in the fridge for 20 minutes.

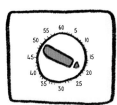

8 Peel, chop and then boil the sweet potato for 10 minutes.

9 Put the cooked sweet potato into a beaker with the cocoa powder, vanilla extract and icing sugar. Blitz with a stick blender until smooth.

10 Trim the top off the cakes so that they are flat, (keep the cake cut-offs for later). Remove the baking paper and sandwich the cakes together with the potato icing.

11 Mix the sugar, cocoa powder, cornflour, water, vanilla extract and butter in a saucepan over a gentle heat. Keep stirring until smooth and slightly thickened.

12 Carefully pour the hot chocolate sauce over the cake and allow to set.

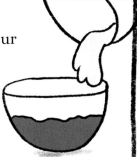

13 Make little stalks out of the marzipan then, stick a raspberry on top. Hollow out the strawberries and stick stalks into these too.

14 Crumble up the cake cut-offs and sprinkle on top of the cake as soil. Add the raspberry and strawberry "mushrooms" and stick in the sprigs of mint. Make little marzipan creatures too!

Ingredients

Cake

115g caster sugar

70g unsalted butter (cubed, at room temperature)

3 large eggs

150g ground almonds

50g self-raising flour

1 tsp almond extract

1 small carrot (about 50g)

150g frozen raspberries

Icing

75g caster sugar

30g cocoa powder

20g cornflour

90ml water

1 tsp vanilla extract

10g unsalted butter

Decoration

12 chocolate buttons

Frozen raspberries

Silver balls (without gelatine)

12 mini pretzels

Makes 12 cakes

WINTER REINDEER PUDS

These sticky puds are perfect if you're having a festive party. No one can resist a Santa's little helper cake!

Method

1 Preheat oven to 180°C (fan-assisted).

2 Whisk the sugar and butter in a mixing bowl.

3 Add the eggs and keep whisking (it will look curdled, but don't worry).

4 Stir in the ground almonds, flour and almond extract.

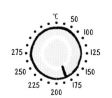

5 Finely grate the carrot and mix this through.

6 Grease a 12-hole muffin tray with butter and drop 3–4 frozen raspberries into each hole.

7 Spoon the mixture equally into the holes.

8 Bake for 15 minutes.

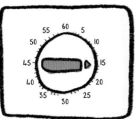

9 Allow to cool on a cooling rack upside down and make a start on your icing.

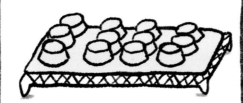

10 Mix the sugar, cocoa powder, cornflour, water, vanilla extract and butter in a saucepan over a gentle heat.

11 Keep stirring until smooth and slightly thickened (if it goes lumpy, take it off the heat and whizz it with a stick blender).

12 Carefully remove the puds from the baking tray. Pour the hot chocolate sauce over the cakes.

13 Cut the chocolate buttons in half and place them at the top of your cakes for ears.

14 Add a defrosted raspberry for the nose and silver balls for the eyes.

15 Just before serving, snap a pretzel in half and stick into your cake to make antlers!

ABOUT DAVID AND ALICE

David Atherton is the winner of *The Great British Bake Off* 2019. David's first cook book for children, *My First Cook Book: Bake, Make and Learn to Cook,* inspired a generation of young cooks to create healthy, imaginative recipes for their friends and family. David is a food writer and an international health adviser for a charity. He has worked on health programmes around the world and never misses an opportunity to explore a new food culture. David is passionate about ensuring that children grow up as food lovers and understand how to make tasty, healthy food.

Alice Bowsher is a London-based illustrator who works primarily with chunky black ink to create joyful characters, large-scale murals and illustrated sets. The imagery she produces is simple, playful and intriguing, full of quick spontaneous marks.